For Mom and Dad
F.L.

THE TURTLE AND THE ISLAND
Text copyright © 1978 by Barbara Ker Wilson and Donald Stokes
Illustrations copyright © 1990 by Frané Lessac
First published in Great Britain in 1990 by Frances Lincoln Limited, London.
Printed in Hong Kong.
1 2 3 4 5 6 7 8 9 10
First American Edition, 1990

Library of Congress Cataloging-in-Publication Data

Wilson, Barbara Ker, 1929-
    The turtle and the island.

    Summary: Retells the legend of how New Guinea was
made by a great sea turtle, the mother of all sea
turtles.
    [1. Folklore—Papua New Guinea]   I. Lessac, Frané, ill.
II. Title.
PZ8.1.W69Tu   1990   398.24′52792′09953   89-134444
ISBN 0-397-32438-3
ISBN 0-397-32439-1 (lib. bdg.)

The
TURTLE
❧ and the ❧
ISLAND

A Folktale from Papua New Guinea

story retold by Barbara Ker Wilson

with paintings by Frané Lessac

J. B. LIPPINCOTT  NEW YORK

Long, long ago, in the days when turtles had teeth, there
lived a great sea-turtle, the mother of all sea-turtles, who
spent her time swimming about the wide sea
that now people call the Pacific Ocean.

Slowly she swam, feeding on the fishes that lived in
the sea and the plants that grew there, and snapping up
the shellfishes that lurked among the rocks where the sea
bordered the land. She swam from one side of the sea to
the other, to and fro between the lands that bordered
that vast ocean.

She lived in the sea, but she swam both on and below the surface of the water. Above the surface she breathed the clear, fresh air and felt the warmth of the sun. She looked up to the sky and saw the sun by day and the moon by night, and the birds that flew across the ocean from land to land. She looked down into the sea and saw its dark, cold depths.

Sometimes the turtle grew tired of swimming, and she rested just below the surface of the sea, but she often longed to rest in the warmth and sunshine. She thought how pleasant it would be if only there were a piece of land in the middle of the great ocean where she lived.

In a dark, secret cave far below the sea where the turtle swam, there lived a man, and in all that great ocean he was the only man. He had no wife, no children, no tribespeople. The man was lonely, in that cave beneath the sea. His heart was heavy as a stone on the seashore. He was weary of being alone.

One day, as the turtle swam about, she came to a place in the middle of the ocean where a great hill of sand was raised up from the bottom of the sea. The hill was so high that the top of it almost reached above the surface of the ocean.

"If I were to bring more sand to add to this big hill, soon it would rise clear above the water," thought the turtle. "The sun would shine down upon it by day, and it would be a place where I could rest and enjoy the warmth and the clear air when I grew tired of swimming."

So the turtle went to another part of the ocean floor, where she dug up rocks and more sand, and these she brought back to the hill, so that it grew higher and higher. She did this more times than anyone could count. The sun rose and set, the moon waxed and waned day after day, and still the hill grew higher. And at last it became a huge island in the middle of the sea, and the turtle saw that her work was finished.

Then the birds that flew across the ocean from land to land brought seeds of plants and trees and dropped them on the island. Grasses and flowering plants and tall trees sprang up, covering the rocks and sand. It was a beautiful, fertile island, surrounded by the sea that teemed with fishes large and small.

The turtle rested on the sun-warmed ground of the island she had made. No longer did she have to spend her whole life swimming through the wide ocean and resting just below its surface. And although she still swam about as before, she never strayed very far from the island she had made.

One day, she swam down, down into the ocean, much deeper than she had ever swum before. How dark and cold it was down there, far from the light and warmth of the sun!

Suddenly the turtle swam into the dark, secret cave where the man had lived alone for such a long time. The man was overjoyed when the turtle came to him; he begged her to find him a wife who would be his companion and bear children. The turtle felt pity for the man's loneliness. She took him, riding on her strong shell, to the island she had made.

Then she swam across the sea to the nearest land, to a place where a woman stood on the shore, a beautiful woman. She was weeping; like the man, she was lonely. She desired a husband and longed to bear children. So the turtle took the woman back across the sea to the island, and brought her as a wife for the man.

The man and the woman lived together on the island in happiness and peace. They laughed, they played in the sea, sometimes they quarreled, but they never lost the joy in their hearts.

They made children together, beautiful children, and those children had more children, and in this way the island became filled with people, who grew crops and built houses and fished along the seashore.

And in time the island that the great sea-turtle had made became known as New Guinea.